Manuel Lopez Mateos

Labor
&
OTHER WRITINGS

Manuel Lopez Mateos

Manuel Lopez Mateos

Labor
&
Other Writings

M_LM
EDITOR

2019

Copyeditor: Libia Bianibi Lopez-Mateos Cortes

English first edition, 2019
©2019 MLM EDITOR
    Matamoros s/n
    Primera Sección
    Santa María Xadani, Oaxaca.
    C.P. 70125
    México

ISBN: 9781097147106

Bibliographic info:
    Lopez Mateos, Manuel.
    Labor & other writings / Manuel López Mateos — 1a ed.
    viii–60 p. cm.

1. Labor 2. Oaxaca 3. Economy 4. Society 5. Sustainability 6. Wage 7. Environment 8. Garbage I. Lopez Mateos, Manuel, 1945-   II. Título.

All rights reserved, MLM EDITOR

Producido en México
Imprint: *Independently published*

```
Version: Tuesday May 7, 2019 2:23am -05:00
https://labor.mi-libro.club
```

Contents

Preface	vii
Labor	1
Labor (II)	3
Saturday: Math Ed	5
Labor & Human Labor	7
Transformation, Labor & Power	9
Labor & Capital	11
Employee & Employer	13
Saturday: More Math Ed	15
Digression: Proofreaders and Typos	17
Us and the environment. The environment and us?	20
1968: 30 Years Later!	22
Capital & Labor	24

Contents

1968: 30 Years Later!	26
Saturday: How to update math teachers?	29
Skills & Knowledge	32
Dictatorship & Economy	34
Concession & Expropriation	36
Marginality & Development	38
Water on the Moon?	40
Evolution of Concepts?	42
Horizontal & vertical	44
Waste & garbage	46
Water!	48
Oaxaca & Chocolate	50
Saturday: Inductive Reasoning	52
Did The Future Reach Us?	54
As a conclusion	56
References	57
Index	58

Preface

We include in this volume most of the articles published in the newspaper CANTERA from Oaxaca City on the first half of 1998.

Although the common thread is LABOR, a subject that from my viewpoint does not lose its relevance and that continues to be a key point for the vital renewal of the economy and the creation of new social relations, the articles also touch on topics related to Oaxaca, the environment and the popular movement of 1968, as well as some interspersed with the teaching of mathematics and the updating of teachers.

If the reading of these writings provokes in some people the desire to pull one or more ends of the skein, I will consider myself well served.

MANUEL LOPEZ MATEOS
manuel@cedmat.net
Tuesday May 7, 2019

Labor

February 11, 1998

Throughout history, LABOR has been seen more as the ability to be exploited than as a particular characteristic of human expression. Labor has been slave, servile and waged. In all its forms it has served to enrich some and impoverish many. At present there is talk, not only in Mexico but as a global panacea, of the need to generate jobs, to provide **work** to population to overcome poverty.

What's it all about? It is clear that in marginal regions we are particularly affected by the ups and downs of the world economy. We are victims of the illusion that it is cheaper to buy than to produce. Work is seen as a way of earning a salary to barely live. But it so happens that the majority of Oaxacans hold high the concept of **enjoying** our resources: The communities of the Central Valleys, the towns of the so-called Huave zone, the guardians of the precious jungles of the Chimalapas, the inhabitants of the Coast and the nearby mountain ranges, the jealous inhabitants of the Mixteca, the towns of the Isthmus, in short, the group of Oaxacan towns, we better prefer —with **work**— to interact productively with our wealth in a way that preserves it, enjoys it and allows us to live from it.

Two concepts of labor are opposed: one that is employed by those who have the capacity to contract it for their benefit and the other that is exercised of their own free will for the benefit of the community. One provides to live and the other requires living to do so. Wage labor captures the individual and in community work the individual is realized as part of society.

However, by necessity of survival, the individual from the community is attracted to work for other people. What do they find in that work? it is evident, sustenance.

So, what new concept of labor are we talking about? Are we talking about the work of Oaxacans that serves to enrich investors in exchange for a bad way to live?

No, we're talking about the work of Oaxacans so that with investment, whether domestic or foreign, we can preserve resources, build jobs and further our culture of self-respect. So that we learn efficient techniques to manage our wealth and locate ourselves, the Oaxacans, in the concert of progress and well-being that is due to the entire human race.

How can we ensure that the work dedicated to the community is productive work according to the canons of the economy contemporary world? It is a question that has an answer.

The key is the new concept of **labor**.

Labor (II)

February 12, 1998

The concept of labor needs to evolve. To do this, we have to reorder or redefine or revalue concepts such as employment, workday, wage, investment, capital, financing and subsidy. We have to express new relationships between these concepts, we have to define new operations to **overcome** the limited exchange formula of working time for salary; operations and relationships can tell us how to move forward and use labor to achieve a dignified place in society.

But labor is not an individual problem, such as employment would be. Labor in a society must be situated as a core element of **large** binder headings to health, education, employment, money and development. It is necessary to parse and situate the role of the work in the transformation, in the evolution from simple stages to complex stadiums. Thus, our effort to propose a conceptualization of labor that allows to overcome the current stagnation and deterioration of the *economic object*, it will take us to develop the themes of:

a) Skills and knowledge,

b) Labor and status,

c) Land ownership: strugling poverty,

d) Ownership of labor: fighting for a place in society,

e) Ownership of capital: spread of wealth, and

f) Education: a duty for human kind.

Note that we must strive to describe the type of society to which we aspire, and the way in which individuals manifest adherence to that model and participate in its construction. We affirm that it is indispensable that the new conceptualization of work allows us to build lines of action and expression to advance towards an economic practice that will support the evolution of humanity towards a society without poverty. That should be a goal for the next century.

Let's start from the begining, currently it is considered that labor is the activity developed in a working day in a job, for which one earns a salary, part in money and part in benefits. There is a clear element: a job presupposes the existence of an employer with the capacity to pay wages. A working day is thought of as continuous hours of readiness for an activity and is not always carried out as part of a job (the clearest example is the housewife). But is work what is done during a working day? In other words, is there no work outside the so-called working day? and, is everything you do in the workday work? We see a the need to question ourselves about the meaning of labor and the meaning of the product of labor, so it is necessary to incorporate two elements: quality and quantity of work.

Saturday: Math Ed

February 13, 1998

Mathematics is a useful, interesting and fun science. Through deductive reasoning it studies the properties of abstract entities, such as numbers and geometric figures, among others, as well as the relationships between them. It includes topics such as arithmetic, geometry, algebra, calculus, probability, statistics and many other areas of research.

Without breaking them apart, one speaks of pure mathematics when researching a subject only for its theoretical interest, and of applied mathematics when developing tools and techniques to solve specific development or engineering problems, or very theoretical applications in other sciences.

Mathematics appear in all aspects of modern life. When making *tamales* or building a house we use numbers, geometry, measurements and space. When designing precision instruments, developing new technologies and building advanced computers we use more abstract mathematics.

Mathematics arises from the need to measure time and count. Thus, the history of mathematics begins with numbers, form recognition and properties of space and time. The earliest evidence of primitive forms of counting appears as notches in bones and marked pieces of stone and wood. The uses of geometry appear as patterns traced in caves and ceramics. As civilization grew, the field of mathematics evolved, sophisticated numerical systems and basic knowledge of arithmetic, geometry and algebra began to develop.

The growing use of mathematics in modern life does not go hand in hand with an adequate development of teaching methods, in particular there is a great deficiency in training and updating in mathematics of elementary school teachers. The teacher's lack of confidence on the subject to be taught generates anguish that leads to a tense situation during mathematics class and an authoritarian attitude towards doubts raised by his students. As a result, generations of students grow up rejecting mathematics and, in general, the study of science, with the consequent loss of human resources capable of employing contemporary technologies needed in the effective planning and realization of a balanced economic development.

Raising the level of educational institutions is a must, and it's achieved through a strong push to improve the quality of education. The emergency task is to carry out a wide program updating in mathematics for elementary education school teachers.

Labor & Human Labor

February 14, 1998

What is labor? Let's start with an elementary conception: Labor is a human being's capacity to transform nature. The first challenge to the elementary conception is that not only do human beings transform nature, but there are a plethora of living beings that do. Do they also *labor*?

No one will deny that ants *labor* when they build their colony. Nobody will deny that bees labor to build their honeycomb, even the analogy is just, we speak of laborers… and also of drones. The lioness hunts and feeds her offspring, the woodpecker, the otter and a multitude of birds, fish, insects, large and microscopic animals build their shelter, feed their offspring, protect the territory and constitute communities; they *labor*. What is the difference between the work of human beings and that of other living beings? *The Moor* already said it (*The Moor* is the affectionate qualification that his daughters gave to KARL MARX): *what distinguishes the worst master builder from the best bee from the start is that they has built the cell in their head before they builds it in wax* [3, vol I, Part 3, Ch. 7.1]. And how do we know that living beings different from human beings do not plan? Without pretending to evade discussion, I am referring to a book that is easy and pleasant to read: *How*

Man Became a Giant[2]. It illustrates how almost all living beings, except the human being, do their labor in a single *habitat* and how only our species is capable of dominating the elements and, through *will* and *labor*, we manage to transform inhospitable spaces into habitable spaces. Let us recognize, for now, that the ability of human beings to survive in adverse conditions, unlike other living beings, rather than mere will implies the ability to *see in advance*, to know *what you want*, to plan. Human labor, in a first appreciation, is planned. Let us say then that labor is the capacity of the human being to consciously transform nature.

We have taken a good step, we distinguish between labor and human labor. Our theme is human labor and we will refer to it as labor.

How is human labor done, that is, labor? I repeat and point out, because it will be necessary in future references; how is labor done?

How is labor done? Why is labor done? Is labor paid? Do we appreciate the labor we do? Do we appreciate the labor of others? What is the relationship between labor and power? What is it, and what should be the relationship between labor and standard of living? Finally, back to the beginning: What is labor?

Transformation, Labor & Power

February 16, 1998

We temporarily embrace, as an additional step to achieve a new concept of labor, that we are talking about the capacity of the human being to conscientiously transform nature.

Why do we transform nature? In the very first place, be it clearly said, in order to subsist. But simultaneously in the human being, in transforming nature as a merely act of survival, other feelings unfold. What drives us to trace differences? to claim spaces? to exclude or tolerate?

It would appear that along with labor, we human beings build the concept of power. Just as a certain location gave rise to the concept of *point*; just as a shadow or a minimum path on the plain gave rise to the concept of **straight**, *perhaps* the concept of personal security gave rise to the most primary concept of **circle**. More than stargazing, perhaps, it was the very self-security that generated the concept of *around*. Labor, power, security, geometry? these were concepts that would not be awkward to see intermingled in the genesis of humanity.

Labor, power, knowledge or science. It seems an appropriate framework for analysis.

In the context of human labor, that is, labor, we must consider similarities and differences between paid and unpaid labor. When an individual is unemployed, it means that the work they do is unpaid, or that their natural willingness, as a human being, to do is restricted. MARX has made deep and interesting analyses about paid work and its relationship with the employer, which we will take up or quote in due course. The core of it is that in wage labor the worker in possession of that good —the capacity to work— exchanges their willingness to subordinate themselves to a certain production process —a workday— in exchange for the sustenance necessary to maintain that ability. During the workday, the worker stops living their life and lives the life of the production process to which they have been assigned. At the end of the day, the worker returns to be themselves. The worker, as an individual, ceases to be so during the workday and returns to be so when the workday is over. This description of Marx's work is called *Estranged Labor*. It is a labor in which the product of work does not belong to the one who does it. The one who performs the work is given what is essential for them to continue performing it, but they do not share in the ownership of the product of their work. Here is a fundamental point in the new conceptualization of work! Whoever performs work or *labor* must participate in the ownership of what they produce!

Labor & Capital

February 18, 1998

It's easy to say: a crucial point in the new conception of labor is that whoever does it must participate in the ownership of what they produce!

Before proceeding further, let us point out that we are now dealing with only one aspect, wage labor. The issue is that the individual should not stop being in their workday to return to being themselves when it ends. The focus, for the time being, is that in the workday the individual should be themselves. They should not rent out their labor capacity and should not cease to be themselves when engaged in a workday. The issue is that the individual should be fulfilled as such during their workday. We affirm that an incentive (an incentive, that is why we mention the subject as an aspect of the liberation from alienated work) will be that whoever makes a day's work participates in the ownership of what is produced.

However, unlike work done *motu propio*, outside the employee–employer relationship, in the workday the ability to perform work is not the only component. There are tools and machinery that are not owned by the user in which the ability is applied. There is investment, in as well as machines, there are buildings and raw materials that are subject to transformation. There exist Capital! From the employer's perspective, the participation in the ownership of the product made during the working day is to be rejected. «They are my machineries, I bought the raw material, the warehouse is mine,» the employer would say, and he would continue: «How are you going to own something that you didn't invest in,» «Ah!» Replied the worker, «You are the owner of the objects with which I work and the material that I transform, but I am the owner of the work capability,» «Correct,» says the employer, «that's why I pay you to work.» «It's true, you pay to work, but you don't pay **The Work**.» «Of course» would add the employer, «I pay you to come, within a certain time, to transform what I put at your disposal, it is called **wage**.»

What happens in the previous conversation? The employer claims what has become habit since labor went from being servile to being waged, that the owner of the means of production exchanges with the *free* wroker is wages for the ability to transform the means during a workday. This is the prevailing conception of the relationship between wage labour and capital. And it's in this relation that we propose a change, an evolution, a new conception, a new viewpoint that both the owners of the capital and the owners of the work force assume.

Employee & Employer

February 19, 1998

What is the new perspective that both capital owners and the labor force owners should adopt? For capital is not only made up of the means of production, but labor is a component of capital (that is, labor is now regarded as a means of production) and wages are only a part (an advance) of the profits investors (the owners of the means of production and labor) will obtain when they complete the natural cycle of production: selling the product, thus opening up a major theme of examination, namely, what is the price of the product? how much of the price corresponds to each component of capital? This problem will be addressed in due course, it is not something simple, it requires calculations from new conceptions of the new value of goods.

We enter in thorny parts, several clarifications are necessary.

To the issues raised from the beginning of these sections there has already been a historical and easy answer: capital is necessary, not the capitalists. The conclusion, which at one stage of history seemed right, is that capital should be social property. It was stated that the means of production should pass from being private to being social property —it was not a bad idea although it was incomplete, since labor was not considered a means of production. The idea established that if the means of production were to be social property, the social property of production would be guaranteed (a not so direct syllogism, but let's concede). The implementation of the idea was disastrous, the worst derivation of political activity intervened in the economic conception: power.

Power has so many facets! No one questions the power that rises against despotism. Nothing is more praiseworthy than power against oppression! And there is nothing more despicable than the power that, in the name of the principles that made it so, is exerted on those who exalted it.

Perhaps, if we manage to properly conceptualize labor, the process of production and how the components of the most diverse processes of production are to be related in a clear way, we can lay effective foundations so that human beings manage to erase the separation between capital and labor. This would link the ownership of capital to the propagation of well-being and the ability to carry out labor while looking for a place in society.

To this end, both employees and employers will have another idea of what they own and will seek to inter-relate in such a way that, in addition to their own benefit, a higher one is contemplated: the benefit of society.

Saturday: More Math Ed

February 20, 1998

On the previous *Saturday*, there was not enough emphasis on saying that mathematics is a useful, interesting and fun science. It is the lack of appropriate math instruction for teachers of elementary education that causes the distress that leads to a tense class and an authoritarian attitude whenever doubts are raised by the students. As a result, generations of children grow up rejecting mathematics and, in general, the learning of science, with the resulting loss of **human resources that use contemporary technologies** essential for effective planning and balanced economic development. We mention the importance of updating elementary education math teachers periodically, which should not be restricted to *updating* them with respect to recent curricular changes, but rather to providing them with the ability to face these changes.

When training and updating teachers, they must be taught in a similar way to how they will teach: exploring, conjecturing and reasoning.

Schoolteachers need to understand the historical evolution and current applications of mathematics. Moreover, they must be acquainted with the power of technology, and they must embrace the rational use of calculators.

Saturday: More Math Ed

In training and updating teachers it is necessary to highlight the following trends in teaching [1].

a) Verifying through logic and mathematical evidence, instead of assuming that the teacher is the only authority to give correct answers;

b) Mathematical reasoning, rather than simply memorizing procedures;

c) Emiting conjectures, development of ingenuity and problem solving, instead of persisting in mechanically searching for answers;

d) Relating and connecting mathematics, its ideas and applications, rather than treating mathematics as an isolated body of concepts and procedures.

Any process of updating must have a beginning. The best way to begin is by addressing the topic of *How to Raise and Solve Problems*, with the study of GEORGE PÓLYA's famous book[2]. Clarity on the following topics is desirable: Exploration with Patterns, Mathematics and Problem Solving, and Using Calculator as a Problem Solving Tool.

Investment in training math teachers will never be in vain. The first beneficiaries will be our daughters and sons. With them, society.

---

[1] [1] BILLSTEIN, R. SHLOMO, L., LOTT, J. W. *A Problem Solving Approach to Mathematics for Elementary School Teachers.*

[2] [4] GEORGE POLYA, *How to Solve it!*

Digression: Proofreaders and Typos

February 23, 1998

It is worth pausing and commenting on the proofreaders and so-called goblins who modify words in articles that change their meaning.

The product of a printed medium, be it a book, a periodical or a newspaper, has to go through stages ranging from the production of content by authors, analysts, reporters, photographers, trainers and proofreaders (to name a few).

Although we still have the amazing technology of fax, e-mail and computer production, there are people who deliver their written material in a traditional typewriter, and people who deliver it by handwriting, rejecting all kinds of technology! Respectable.

The risk is that the material presented for publication passes through many hands, sometimes the typist makes a mistake (it is called a finger error), in another step someone, supposedly widely read, *polishes* the material by removing excess articles, changing repeated words and, in general, improving the submitted text. That's good! It's good to improve articles, polish essays and coherently present ideas. In this regard, when in spite of the meticulousness in caring for the quality of the final product, the product intended for thousands of readers, an erratum escapes or a modification that alters the meaning appears, the fault is usually attributed to a mischievous goblin who lives in the editorial tables of (in this case) newspapers.

While irritating to the author, it is clear how hard it is to succeed in a process where so many hands are involved. When the author of a note, article or report reads modifications to its version, they usually (hurt) blames the famous goblin for the mischief.

Computer technology came to the aid of the troubled author (and many others), applied not only to complicated calculations. Until recently it was believed that computers would only aid accounting, financial and engineering processes. The development of computer science made its goodness available to other disciplines, and the use of computers quickly spread to design, mainly engineering, and later to publishing design.

Computing caught up with the office and today we see powerful computers used as typewriters. An advantage of writing journal articles on a computer is that you don't have to retype them, you submit the content on a disc and from there it is incorporated into the publication design.

Why, then, do the goblins keep making their changes? I believe it's not goblins but excessively energetic proofreaders who change, for example, the fine concept of *around* to explain the possibility of human expression in the sphere of personal security, expressed in last Wednesday's column, by the *rodent* noun[3].

What did the proofreader think? Did they think that *around* was not a word? Let's give them the benefit of the doubt! But

---

[3] In *Spanish* the words for *around* (*rededor*) and *rodent* (*roedor*), although they resemble each other, they have very different meanings.

Digression: Proofreaders and Typos

why did they think that the word to describe the personal sphere of security should be *rodent*? That's really puzzling.

Another example, on the first *Saturday* on mathematics education, our active proofreader decided that the sentence that, in my humble opinion, was the reason for the article was superfluous, namely, that the significant depletion of human resources capable of employing contemporary technologies was the product of the current crisis in mathematics education. How do you fix it? With a weekly summary of errata?

Perhaps, and for sure, it is better that the proofreaders do not let the goblins through (jokingly).

Us and the environment. The environment and us?

February 24, 1998

It would appear that environmental issues do not touch us on a personal level. It would seem that when we are talking about the environment we are talking about speeches from groups removed from our most immediate concerns. There has been talk of ecological damage caused by the northern beltway in the Oaxacan Central Valleys, there has been talk of shrimp mortality caused by Salineras companies in the Isthmus of Tehuantepec, there has been talk of the desforestation of the Chimalapas and other jungles and forests, there has been talk of hazardous waste industries, there has been talk that we Oaxacans are on the verge of ecological disaster. We, with such wealth... and yet so far away.

How can we, on a personal level, participate in solving so many complex problems? Among so many ways of involvement we have a main one: garbage management. Until not so many years ago it was a delight, both for locals and tourists, to walk through the villages of the Central Valleys. Walk along the roads and reach one town, then another. Maybe visit acquaintances, participate in a local celebration, certainly bringing guests and showing them the cultural and physical beauty of the surroundings. The same thing happened when we walked proudly along the coast, or on the way to Huajuapan, or towards Tuxtepec. But what is happening now? It seems that the sign for a village is a pile of disposable dipers. Few, very few communities can be proud of their image of cleanliness. You don't have to go far, we can walk outside, by the green Antequera and see lots of garbage

What happened to us?

Why aren't we embarrassed to throw a plastic bag in the street?

Why do we throw garbage bags anywhere?

When did we lose self-respect?

There is an easy-answer: the Government is not providing sufficient clean-up facilities. Is life in society then, the result of the government's will?

Oaxacan culture is not so recent. It is an ancient culture, we are proud (truly proud?) descendants of people with advanced scientific knowledge, with delicate aesthetic conception, with elaborate architectural knowledge. What made us throw garbage in the streets and get dirty? The economic crisis, they say. It's true, we had a crisis in the economy of each one of our families as we haven't felt for a long time. But no crisis should undermine our dignity. We must fight the economic crisis and its causes. But we need to know how to fight while preserving dignity and health.

Let us prevent our villages from being flooded with garbage!

1968: 30 Years Later!

February 25, 1998

February 1968. Thirty years ago in the DF[4], in Mexico City, there was an ambience of renewal. The issue that had been dealt with for a couple of years was the so-called Generational Conflict. In the world, of course also in Mexico, young people were shaken by the authoritarianism that marked their lives: parents, teachers and authorities, censorship, omnipotence and omniscience of government and institutions. At that time even the most ignorant traffic cop was clothed with the most dignified authority using his peculiar logic. Years later, the incoherent way of expressing oneself was called the *traffic cop's logic*.

It was the time when people went to university in suits, or at least in cashmere pants (perhaps with a tie). It was a time when the UNAM was fighting against the Societies of Students managed by the authorities via the violence of the MURO[5] and was successful at winning elections in polling places properly guarded.

Surely it was in that couple of years prior to 1968, when the students finally voted without fear, when they managed to

---

[4] *Distrito Federal* (Federal District), old name of *Ciudad de México, CDMX*.
[5] *Movimiento Universitario de Renovadora Orientación* (University Movement of Renewal Orientation), a far right student organization.

assert the will expressed in ballot boxes, and in stormy sessions of vote recounts they got rid of the MURO, surely it was in those years that the will that made possible July 16, 1997 was generated[6].

But it was not the only thing that came out. The expressions of the so-called generational non-conformity of those years forged the best manifestations that today are proposing a new vision of our beloved country, and sometimes so, but so distant.

In that atmosphere of searching for freedom, artistic expressions; criticism and proposals, literary boom and scientific production; in that critical and festive environment, in that moment of healthy expression solidarity with just causes —like the pacific demonstration of July 26, 1968 supporting the Cuban Revolution— were repressed with unprecedented brutality.

After the emergency, in schools and faculties of the *Poli*[7] and the UNAM, a call to session was made at the General Assembly of Students, the organ that allowed them to face, for years, authoritarian impositions and attacks by groups of beaters.

We already know how the government reacted. But between the July 26, 1968 repression and the October 2, 1968 massacre, things happened: The most despised and scorned entity by the government manifested itself: society.

---

[6] When the ruling party, PRI, lost the majority in the Chamber of Deputies.

[7] Short for *Instituto Politécnico Nacional* (National Polytechnic Institute).

Capital & Labor

February 26, 1998

A major component in the conceptualization of labor announced in previous columns is the relationship between the individual and society. You may have noticed the recurring reference to society!

In summary, when dealing with wage labor, we affirm that whoever works must participate in the ownership of the product of his labor. We also point out the indisputable role of capital in the production process. In this regard MARX pointed out that he saw the need for capital in the process of production but did not see the need for the existence of capitalists. This statement was interpreted as the need to expropriate capital and turn the means of production into social property. The famous and feared phrase of **the abolition of private property** meant that capital —or the means of production— should not be owned by a few, hence the inference that it should be socially owned and (in a forced conclusion) that the expropriated means of production should become administered by the State. Past historical experience has shown the error of such a conception.

Indeed, the scheme of capital accumulation (that is, the ownership of the means of production) in a few hands on one side, and the exploitation (paying for a day's labor without sharing the ownership of the product) of masses owning only labor force on the other side, besides unfair leads to economies of recurrent crises. It facilitates the construction of social green houses —where those who knew how to step on others enjoy their standards of living— and social garbage dumps formed by masses of the unemployed and marginalized, a population with the acquired sense of taking advantage of others, where crime appears to be a better way to live than work. This scheme divides society, confronts it with its interior and breaks its solidarity pact, dividing and winning.

How to modify the scheme with the involvement of all of its constituents? Let's modify the concept of labor. Let us modify the employment–employer relationship. Instead of expropriating capital, let us all participate in its ownership. We know that a fundamental characteristic of capital is to reproduce. Let us participate in it! In fact we must reproduce capital, even more so if we participate in its ownership. Who can be against that? It's a matter of doing the math. Today there are avant-garde conceptions about participating in companies by investing in labor. At least two things are required: efficient management of the means of production and capable exercise of the laborforce.

1968: 30 Years Later!

February 27, 1998

The ferocious repression of that demonstration on the occasion of the anniversary of the Cuban revolution was very disconcerting, but things like that happened. What came out of the scheme was the disproportionate intervention of the police forces in a rift between two schools. Unlike the government's position that a great plot against Mexico was being prepared, from the student side it was perceived that such great plot against Mexico was being plotted by the government itself, and so it happened.

There is much to tell of the many events that happened from July to October 1968 starting with the huge social movement created in response to the repressive deployment of governmental force —that had consequences we still suffer today–, but in the great plot against Mexico conceived by the government, a major objective was dismantling higher education.

UNAM and POLI, indisputably, formed the professionals of Mexico. And to talk about the professionals of Mexico, trained from the 20's or 30's until the 60's, was to talk about the formation of avant-garde personalities in their fields, with a deep humanist formation and a broad culture and Renaissance thought, generous and risky characters in their conceptions.

Formators, disseminators of advanced ideas and leaders of teams made up of their students.

After '68, and until recently, administrators, not the avant-garde, were advancing, and a greasy layer of unpleasant individuals began to lead.

Those who held power could not replace the cadres they were trying to displace and for it they made monsters of administration (if my friend does not know, let him manage!) The example spread. Ways of managing things instead of doing things flourished throughout the country. Today we see administrators everywhere (administration is not bad, but you need some real thing to manage). Today everyone wants to trade (who produces?) So much trade! So much administration! Who's going to work?

Values have been disrupted, it is better to pretend than to do. The damage is done. Today, outside very few public education institutions, and even outside some POLI and UNAM schools, in many higher education institutions, public and private, certified of excellence, the rite of connivance is fulfilled: the teacher pretends to teach and the student pretends to learn. Don't move, don't make waves. Teaching ceased to be that effort to form better people. Learning now, just as the count at a polling place, lacks credibility.

There was damage. The generations before '68, the young people of the '60s, in addition to what was reported in the press and thoughtful analysis, participated in an incredible passion for study. The avant-garde of the time *shrank* and the mediocre advanced.

This was part of the great triumph of the government's conspiracy against Mexico. The big, huge question is: Why did they do it?

Contemporary Mexico having overcame those traumas with its vigor, told us what we could have done and who could we have been a long time ago. But it's never too late and what wasn't can be now, maybe not as we thought thirty years ago —surely, the problems are more complex. Society will still have to recompose its internal social pact, but we can move forward. We can put ourselves together or simply march on and perhaps say: **Thirty years is nothing!**

PostData: After thirty years I keep asking myself why? Why destroy that humanist, educated, cosmopolitan, egalitarian Mexico that seemed our destiny? Why is now the time for racists, classists, uneducated, and exclusionary?

Saturday: How to update math teachers?

February 28, 1998

The task is huge. We have three issues to think about, the first is that the updating task is for teachers in service, not for the recently finished with their formative stage that are not very skilled in adapting to new curricula. The second point is that they are many teachers widespread, not only in the Oaxaca case, in distant territories. The third point is that updating plans designed by the SEP[8], only give methodological indications, and seek efficiency in the management of a class.

In no case do the updating plans for teachers that the SEP constitutes, equips elementary school teachers to face the inevitable evolution of curricula.

The big flaw is that the alleged updating plans go a step behind, they want to teach teachers how to teach the new curricula, when those who teach elementary mathematics would do better participating in a long-term updating plan that would make them proficient in the materials. This would enable them to cope with any changes.

---

[8] *Secretaría de Educación Pública* (Secretary of Public Education).

Saturday: How to update math teachers?

Updating by only giving methodological indications from teachers will always fail. However, if an ambitious plan were implemented to equip teachers with the ability to comprehend the subject matter they teach and actually train them as teachers with a certain level of knowledge they could handle; if they were trained to lessen their anguish when faced with children willing to learn, express doubts, and ask a myriad of questions; if teachers were trained to lead discussions and resolve doubts, we would surely have generations prone to the study of science.

Let us not speak badly of teachers dedicated to elementary education. Those who know the problems of elementary education must understand the degree of dedication and commitment that those devoted to such a noble endeavor surely have.

In no way is it thought that teachers of elementary education are responsible for the hatred that children feel for mathematics and, in general, for science. The responsibilities lie with the people who are supposed to provide them with updating processes.

How to carry out a real process of updating in mathematics elementary schoolteachers (and let us include those of secondary education) that are actively working?

Although it is necessary a state-wide program (or national) to update elementary school teachers in mathematics, we do no think that it should be thought and executed at once. You have to learn, you can't go from nothing to everything. That's why we propose a two-week pilot plan to weigh successes and shortcomings.

Television[9] should be used as the main medium. In-person courses in important locations would require absurd trips by

---

[9] Now we should say Internet, instead TV

interested teachers. Television programming could even be recorded and become reference material. Written material would be available that the participants would answer, send and receive back corrected. It is a test that we must do. **The issue is not political, it is academic!**

Skills & Knowledge

March 9, 1998

We have argued that a good direction for evolving the concept of labor requires that whoever works participates in the ownership of the product of labor, and that applying such a concept requires the consent of both the owners of the means of production and the owners of the labor force. It is a new way of understanding production and benefiting from the process!

We said it was a matter of doing the math. Both participants in the production process must do the math, we must find the point of common benefit. The equitable position is: the owner of the means of production expects to make a profit from their investment and the owner of the workforce expects to make a profit from their investment.

We have made it clear that the wage perceived by the worker is only a fraction, the essential part for living, of that which corresponds to him. It is obvious that the owner of the means of production would never be satisfied with the proceeds from the sale of the commodities being enough just to maintain the machinery, no! They expects a profit, an extra, they hopes to recoup their investment and get more: the profit. The other party, the worker, has to expect the same.

Let's be clear, we are not speaking against labor, but against work only to live. It is legitimate for each participant in the production process to aspire to a certain comfort, to see that with their work they can achieve personal fulfillment. How is it possible for the worker to share in the profits?

Although I have previously warned that the answers to a myriad of questions posed here will be the product of several and diverse investigations, we can illustrate the arguments with well-known examples.

Perhaps the best known example of sharing ownership of the work product are the royalties (percentage of sales) obtained by the author of a book. This is how it works: someone who writes a book, called the author, gets an advance from the publisher that will publish it, this could be the part comparable to the wage: a little money that serves to pass it on; the book goes on sale, each copy sold corresponds to the author a percentage of the sale price (varies between 20% and 30%). The amount in royalties will depend on whether many copies are sold, and quickly, or if the book is sold slowly but steadily.

The question raised, about the participation in the ownership of the product of labor, could be summed up in How to make workers obtain *royalties* from the product of their labor?

Dictatorship & Economy

March 10, 1998

Getting *royalties* from the labor product is a very nice concept, but in order to achieve this, the labor must also be of good quality and the product must be a commodity that is realized in the market, that is sold.

This is where we come into crisis with an aspect of the current model of merchandise production: a bad product with good advertising is sold. A good product with bad marketing is not sold. As the market becomes saturated and the merchandise has to fight each other for customers, not only does it sell advertising, but it must also be accompanied by (big surprise!) *quality*. Now the economical geography intervenes, there are zones of the planet in which the remainders of other zones are sold. There are areas made up of captive customers of companies that, in addition to being highly polluting, produce articles of poor quality, expensive and ugly!

Such companies are not interested in improving their productivity nor will they allow laborers to participate in the ownership of their work, rather they will pay the lowest possible wages with high exploitation of the labor force, those areas are oppressed societies, where popular struggles do not even pose strategic improvements in the economy but struggle to shake

Dictatorship & Economy

off a dictatorship. Such libertarian struggles against dictatorial oppression have often been confused (or attributed to them) with movements that propose new economic schemes. The question arises from three observations, first: Many times it is enough for an oppressed society to get rid of the oppressor and enter into an economic practice based on the *free* exchange of wages for labor, second: Along with the liberation of the oppressed society, collectivizing schemes of the economy are proposed, the workers obtain their additional gain to the salary through social benefits that for a good time serve as an emergency plan in disaster zone, equitable policies are put in place especially in the sectors of health and education, the wounds caused by the dictatorship begin to heal and society aspires to participate more in the economy. Collectivization becomes paternalism and starts to get narrow. Society magnifies the concept of private enterprise and more than workers with fair participation, they think of being, all of them, entrepreneurs. The third observation is still utopia: Perhaps in marginalized societies, or in the recent emergence of antidictatorial struggles, it is possible to begin, albeit in an elementary way, production with effective participation in the ownership of the product of labor.

But it is in the advanced enterprise where it is easier to put into practice the evolved conception of work.

Concession & Expropriation

March 11, 1998

Commentaries on dictatorships and economics illustrated three ways, two historical and one utopian, of an economic evolution of a society recently shaken by a dictatorship. There are, however, currently marginalized societies for which it is possible to evolve their economy according to the new concept of labor, I mean societies where the *collective enjoyment of resources* is rooted. In these societies, the practice of granting concessions for the exploitation of their resources is common: a company with powerful capital (and sometimes not so much) exploits the resources of a community and, in return, it gives a job! paying wages, although higher than those obtained in the area, without the community's participation, or of the workers themselves in the ownership of the production.

To be paid with the opportunity to receive a salary in exchange for exploiting the resources of a community seems to me to be the crudest form of the old-fashioned employer-employee relationship and, of course, easy to be overcome through the application of the new concept of labor. Moreover, in the concession of exploitation of resources can be given, more clearly, the participation of society in the work and their benefits.

The most outrageous example of how a good chance to participate in economic development (and apply a novel conception of participation with ownership of land and work) becomes the dispossession of goods from a community and throwing a population to the marginalization, is the tourist development of Huatulco bays.

The conditions for touristic development in Huatulco bays ranked number one in the country, followed by Cancun and Los Cabos. At that time the development of Cancun was given preference because the infrastructure for Huatulco was almost nil. Finally, the great step was taken to make Huatulco, as well as a first class tourist center, an alternative of great urban development. Good project! But why should the landowners have to be dispossessed of their land? They could not participate as investors, as owners? They did not have money, it was said, but those who were given land did not have it either! Finally, it was not intended that the communities owning the land would also be the investors and owners of the grand tourism hotels, but that they would participate, to the extent of their investment, in this case the ownership of the land, in the benefits and responsibilities of this great project.

It so happened that the new concept of labor was not enforced.

Marginality & Development

March 12, 1998

Paradoxically, it is in some marginalized societies and advanced enterprises where it is easier to put the new concept of labor into practice. We have already mentioned, as an illustration, how the author shares the royalties for the sales of their work.

Marginalized societies where it is possible to make a social pact that allows the *collective enjoyment* of resources, and by social pact I mean that such collective enjoyment is part of their culture, not a desire for collectivization, are prone to understand participation in labor and profits, not only in the exploitation of resources but in enterprises with third-party means of production.

In advanced enterprises, especially in highly industrialized countries, in branches that require a high level of creativity and responsibility in production, the phenomena of involving workers in the ownership of the enterprise through the allocation of shares is already beginning to occur. Not by involving workers in the ownership of the company does it diminish its profits or cease to be attractive to other capital investors.

In tackling the issues we are dealing with, we must address the problems of the employer, not just those of the employee.

It is not so easy to be an employer, especially if you are an entrepreneur, someone with good ideas and little money.

Let's take a look at the other side of the coin. The production process is organized, it barely complies with wages and benefits, and with a small plant of employees with little capacity and no culture of responsibility with the work, it soon sees its production compliance dates exceeded, the merchandise does not go out to the market, it is placed in insolvency, the employees sue it, bankruptcy, and...end of the project. What could have been a life alternative for a group of people frustrates.

Such a description is not uncommon. It illustrates a fundamental element: responsibility to labor. It is not enough to pretend to participate in the product of labor, there must be a product, and it must be good, and it must be sold! Claiming to share ownership of the product forces you to share responsibility for production. The owner of the means of production, as we said here recently, must be efficient in the management of the means of production, and the worker must be capable and efficient in the development of their labor.

The owner of the means of production makes a mistake by not wanting to make the worker share in the ownership of the work product. And the worker makes a mistake by claiming ownership of a product that cannot be made as a commodity. (Neither you, nor me. GARCÍA LORCA.)

Water on the Moon?

March 13, 1998

Late last week we awakened with a piece of news that, if true, will certainly alter the course of space research: Water has been found on the Moon!

The news was that the probe in orbit around the Moon detected some ice flakes in the depths of shady craters. However, authoritative sources asserted that the existence of a water supply for modest earth colonies, sufficient for several centuries, could be inferred from this. It was also said that the amount of hydrogen on the Moon would allow refueling of expeditions to more distant places.

Sounds good! as an anticipation of exploration. Just imagine, perhaps the biggest obstacle to establishing a colony on the Moon is the water supply, but now there seems to be enough, for several centuries, for a modest colony.

My concern is about how many centuries the water supply on planet Earth will last for the modest colony that inhabits it, called humans; but I am wrong, because not only humans consume water on this planet. How long will the water supply on planet Earth last for the modest colony that inhabits it, called living beings?

Calculations are already being made about the amount of water available on the Moon, as well as the way in which the glaciers that seem to be on Mars will melt and thus be able to generate an atmosphere (as in the film).

I would like to know how the calculations are going to rehabilitate polluted water on planet Earth, and not just water, let's remember that a few years ago the planet was considered in danger of extinction, and illustrated, on the cover of a magazine, with a plastic wrap instead of atmosphere. The bad news is that in order to rehabilitate polluted water and to stop the deterioration of the planet, calculations are not enough, the action of those of us who call ourselves conscious beings is necessary.

We already know the great responsibility that weighs on industries and governments. We also know of signed agreements: Agenda 21, the Earth Summit, among others. There are responsibilities and it is perhaps the most powerful economic and political groups that carry the largest ones. Many civil organizations around the world try to oppose the arrogant attitude of indifference of the modern predators of the planet.

However, the lack of individual consciousness is a concern. What do we have to do? Surely there is a task of our concern: to learn how to handle our waste.

We must stop generating garbage.

Even if there is water on the Moon.

Evolution of Concepts?

March 23, 1998

Many comments have been made on the new concept of labor. Both in employees and in employers the question arises: how to do it? how, on one side (from the employer), to make the worker participate in the ownership of their work, without bankrupting in the attempt? and, on the other, how is it going to be possible to start earning more than the salary received, how without working more?

Clearly, we need to formalize what this new concept of labor means. As we have already mentioned, there are a couple of evident things: The employer should have an efficient production process, should strive to attain product quality and competitiveness, and the employee should participate in the production process with the same attitude as the media owner. This should be clear. It should be explained in a meaningful way in an in-depth analysis. For the time being, we are using informal and, let us admit, somewhat unclear language. On the one hand we distinguish between the owner of the means of production and, on the other hand, we say that work is also a means of production. As we move forward, actors, roles, concepts and relationships become clearer. Not only this, but the main point: the operations that will clear, both quantita-

Evolution of Concepts?

tively and qualitatively, in a satisfactory way, the contributions of each participant.

We also received comments about the futility or impossibility of constructing a new concept of labor. «Labor is the way it is,» —they tell me, «you labor, I pay you, and that's it.»

I have to stress the importance of improving the concept of labor. Remember: There were concepts that made the Earth the center of the universe; later it was thought that it was the Sun; now we have a conception of the Universe as a product of an explosion, it expands and we do not know if it will continue like this or at a given moment it will begin to shrink. There are several conceptions. Also it was believed, when it was possible to calculate with accuracy the movement of the Sun and its planets, that everything was being said about the study of the movement of bodies, a notion which saw its limitations in not being able to solve the famous problem of the three bodies. Something similar happened with the notions of space and time. Finally, we can see how concepts that describe the physical world around us evolve.

What about the concept of labor? Apparently, the concept of exchanging labor for wages is obsolete. We have reached the impasse with no apparent way out of the macroeconomic crises. Could it be that the economy has become an old science, and requires a fresh bath of new concepts?

Might it not be that we have to seek a new idea of labor?

Horizontal & vertical

March 24, 1998

Other commentaries are critical of the presentation approach used in these writings: «Stop branching around and get to the point.»

It is noteworthy to draw the difference between research and exposure methods.

When, as is the case, we pursue a new conceptualization, it happens that interventions are made as if one *thought aloud*; one releases ideas, sketches relationships, issues conjectures, tests affirmations, orders and prioritizes, arranges actors, thinks about possible hypotheses (therefore plausible), weighs the desired conclusions and analyzes their feasibility, modifies them and adapts them, in the train of thought, to others that seem demonstrable. In short, it is the creation process.

It is a different matter when the work is finished. The hypotheses are enunciated, their pertinence is exhibited, and the conclusion is logically deduced, which will now have the status of an indisputable law or principle.

The ideas expressed in these writings are part of an effort to achieve a new conceptualization of the work, it is —I repeat— an effort performed publicly.

I am *thinking out loud* in front of all of you, the readers.

If the whole new concept of labor that I have in mind were complete, round, finished, instead of going to the trouble of reading what is new every day, you could look at a voluminous (would it be voluminous or would it only come to a pamphlet?) and pompously bound volume that would be the new manual of Labor.

We all know that there are many loose ends in the process of investigation. Completed research is a sound presentation.

Mention the above since we are used to have a true referent. It can be a proven theory, or a certain ideology.

If we are talking about proven theories, especially in the field of the physical world, it is simple; we refer to the appropriate law and verify if our conjecture is fulfilled or not.

It is far more complex when ideology is involved. Instead of knowledge, ideology is belief. People who participate in ideologies do not interact with other human beings through exchanging opinions, but by comparing the other' s thoughts with a preconceived idea. The relationship between human beings, rather than based on the mutual scrutiny of ideas, refers to the search for a possible fit of other people's points of view in certain schemes, and even in known writings. Instead of horizontal, the interaction between human beings is mediated by a superior referent: a written text, a belief, the taste of a boss or the thought of a leader.

Waste & garbage

March 25, 1998

We already mentioned that we have a task: To learn how to handle our waste. We have to stop producing garbage.

A means of grading our quality of life is how we dispose of our waste. Waste is one thing and the other is to turn it into a filthy mess.

So let's begin with the place we call the garbage place at home. Usually it's a smelly boat.

Who says that the place where we deposit the garbage should be dirty? What is garbage? How is it that we make of our waste a smelly mess, a source of infections?

Clearly, as a product of everyday life, we produce waste: toilet paper that we don't flush down the drain, watermelon husk, yesterday's newspaper, empty bottle, milk container, shopping pieces that we don't use when cooking, food waste, paper here, a bag there, a box, chicken guts, and more, much more. We throw it all in a bag and throw it in the trash. In the trash? few go to a dumpster or intercept the pickup truck; many simply toss the bag on the way to work, or in the nearby river, or behind the yard. What happens? We turn our waste in filth.

So the question is, what do we do with waste?

Waste & garbage

Let's see: Organic waste such as lettuce leaves we don't eat, radish leaves, chicken guts, egg shells, orange peels, and even our feces are rich in nutrients that should be returned to the soil to maintain its fertility. Of course, no one throws the above in the backyard to re-fertilize the planet. All I would get is plague and fly clouds. But these wastes are actually nutrients that must be returned to the soil. In the countryside, holes can be dug where organic waste can be deposited exclusively, covering them with some soil; after a few months, the best fertilizer will be made available there. And in urban areas there should be this type of *compost*, so called, by neighborhood, without confusing compost with landfill. Really, we should only throw in the garbage car paper and plastic, separated (and that because treating it requires additional effort, for now let's handle organic waste properly).

Think of the large amount of nutrients that instead of returning to the soil, when mixed with plastics produce toxins.

How do we get started? Do not throw with disgust our waste. We must separate them and use them. It's for our benefit.

Water!

March 26, 1998

Last Friday, March 20, the ancient propitiatory rite of water took place in the city of Oaxaca. It was offered, drank.

Water, water, how we miss water. We can still feel the severity of the dryness. Our crops miss the water, our forests and our jungles miss the water. By natural causes (glass transformed into a magnifying glass and a ray of sunshine into a spark, and pasture into an oven), or by imprudence (a cigar, a match, a charcoal grill), or by evil, our forests and jungles catch fire. Drought transforms exuberance into misery. In the great jungle of the Amazon, at this moment, fire sweeps surfaces as large as countries.

Where is the water? Where is the planet's watering hole? Where are forests and jungles, pastures, crops and cities going to quench thirst?

We are used to having water, just like that, water exists and it is enough to open a tap and have it. It would seem that water is there, at our disposal, as it seems that there is electrical light in the city, or the taxi on the corner, or the road to go.

We can understand when there is not a particular fruit since it is not the season, but it would never occur to us to imagine that it is not the electric light season, we must have it. And so we are thinking of water, we always should have it.

We know that the electrical energy we consume is produced by human beings (it would be better for us to know that it is produced by means of water), but how is water produced?

Water is precipitated vapour from the planet's atmosphere, the same vapour that is generated from water heated by the Sun.

From where does the water that the Sun heats come up to evaporate it and then precipitates as rain and water is available? Easy, most of that chemical compound formed by two molecules of hydrogen and one of oxygen, called H_2O by ones and water by us, is dismissed by plants during the day, and absorbed during the night.

When through natural factors or through the intervention of the famous conscious being (called, in equity, human being) the stain of the planet's vegetation is reduced (combined with holes in the ozone layer, which we would have to find out its causes), the water generation capacity is diminished.

Humanity, and all other living beings that inhabit this planet, face a major problem: **it is essential to generate water**.

Of course, you will tell me that it is the government's responsibility, but is our life an act of government? Government has its responsibility and, in due course, will be called upon (as its protest points out). Meanwhile what? Let's act: Let's do an intensive reforestation work. Let's plant trees and see that they grow.

Oaxaca & Chocolate

March 27, 1998

The State of Oaxaca certainly has the ingredients to be an international center for the sciences and the arts. It is well known that visitors to Oaxaca have a strong fondness for culture.

We are also aware that, aside from the rich oil products industry (that doesn't include us), it is the tourism industry that generates a significant benefit to the population.

We Oaxacans should be aware that the beaches are not the only attraction for tourists. Oaxacan Pacific beaches are of great beauty, nobody denies it, rather we celebrate it. However, I would insist that they are not the only tourist attraction. Oaxaca has many other points of interest: Their cultures, cities and towns.

Oaxaca offers diverse ways of life, almost all referring to its old cultures. As an attraction, Oaxaca could offer a way to feel, to study, to coexist, to be part of it. Particularly, the city of Oaxaca would provide a backwater for artistic and scientific research and creation. Their conditions are so that their campuses of higher educational institutions would be of great attraction for the world community of scholars.

The best way to preserve our cultural heritage is to render the condition of humanity's heritage effective through the sharing among us of the finest of human thought!

But we need more than a few efforts. The first one, concerning, so far, the city of Oaxaca, is related with the condition of this city. Admittedly, the attraction of the city is reduced to a few blocks around downtown and Santo Domingo convent. It is scandalous even there the level of pollution. The touristic center, or historical (according to the euphemism), is a roadway crossing place. It is not a destination to be there. They are crossed by roads that those of us who go from one place to another in the city pass through. Oaxaca City's first condition for rehabilitation is that each place worthy of admiration ceases to be a passageway. The whole so-called Historical Center should be closed to vehicular traffic.

But this is not the greatest problem, the big problem of the city of Oaxaca is that it is not a city anymore, but it is conformed by concentric rings of belts of misery. Rather than planning their growth, land occupations have been tolerated in a patronizing manner, to the point of invading one of the most important ceremonial centers of humanity: Monte Alban.

Are we that blind? Are we apathetic or powerless?

Will we allow one of our great riches, the city of Oaxaca, to crumble like bread in chocolate?

Saturday: Inductive Reasoning

March 28, 1998

Scientists do observations and propose general laws that are based on observations and patterns. Statisticians use patterns when drawing conclusions based on collected data. This is **inductive reasoning**, the method of generalizing from observations and patterns [1].

While inductive reasoning can also lead to discoveries, the weakness of inductive reasoning is that the conclusions are drawn only from collected evidence. If not all cases have been verified, there is the possibility that in some other case the conclusions are false.

Inductive reasoning can lead us to **conjecture** a proposition that is thought to be true but that has not been proven to be true or false. For example, based only on $0^2 = 0$ and $1^2 = 1$, we might conjecture that any number squared is equal to itself.

Whenever we find an example that contradicts the conjecture, we have provided a counterexample. To show that the above conjecture is not true, it is sufficient to exhibit at least one **counterexample**, say $2^2 = 4$.

Saturday: Inductive Reasoning

It is sometimes hard to find a counterexample, but not being able to find a counterexample does not mean that the conjecture is true.

PROBLEM Suppose that 6 people participate in a chess tournament, each of them must play a game against each of the other participants. Find the number of games played.

Explore Analyze the situation. Look for an image to help you think.

Discuss Do we see a pattern that shows the number of games depending on the number of players? What does the pattern indicate for 3 people, and for 4 people, and for more people?

When you discover a pattern that seems to work, you have to try it in several cases. If the pattern works for those cases we might think it will work for all cases. This is inductive reasoning: Seeing that a pattern works in several cases invites us to make a guess.

Emitting a conjecture means that we imagine, that we think that our proposal solves the problem. There is, however, to demonstrate that it is so.

Send the solution to the problem. The first correct solution received will be published.

Did The Future Reach Us?

June 1, 1998

The past few weeks have witnessed an environmental crisis without precedent. The city of Oaxaca was wrapped in a thick mist. Many activities were disrupted, most notably air traffic. The people still experience discomfort and damage to the respiratory tract, and the landscape ceased to be one of the most translucent parts of the air (Carlos Fuentes' compliment to the Valley of Mexico), and Oaxaca, from Verde, became IMECA Antequera, with rumored rates of more than 200 points.

We lived for days one of the potential futures of the capital city of the state of Oaxaca.

For the inhabitants of the Central Valleys, the well-known *calina* thickened and a grey, dark layer began to form, preventing the vision of nearby hills and even domes and end of streets. The sun stopped dazzling in the morning, it became a pale ball between orange and yellow painted gray, finally disappeared, its presence perceived behind a less dark spot in the sky. Visitors from Mexico City saw things as normal, nothing seemed out of place, and they were even astonished that the lack of visibility was a comment.

Why was the situation of environmental crisis, what caused the mist, was it something unusual, or is it going to be part of our climate and landscape, can we prevent it?

Did The Future Reach Us?

The questions above are typical expressions of immediate reaction to unforeseen situations, that is, to unexpected and surprising phenomena. Suddenly an unwanted future arrives, but the future does not just happen, it is being built.

If what happened, besides bothering us, surprises us, we would do well to ask ourselves what we expected.

Perhaps for this time of year we would like to celebrate the shortening of the dry season, the first rains almost coincide with the arrival of spring, the soil of the Central Valleys, never completely dry, renews its fertility, the severe green of the hills is given way to the tender green of the offspring, and the stream of the Atoyac distributes, generously, the waters collected in distant mountain ranges, its passage through Oaxaca is observed by the immense trees on its banks. The city of Oaxaca blooms once again, multitude of colors are mixed in the vegetation of its streets and avenues, in its parks and gardens. Its surroundings, as it has grown, have the peaceful atmosphere of the urban outline that balances the room and the green area. The inhabitants celebrate that, once again, it was declared a city free of garbage and a place of high quality of life.

Why not?

How come reality is presented as misfortune after misfortune, disaster after disaster, crisis after crisis, instead of resembling an expected welfare, an attained achievement, and a satisfied need?

Most likely, as a society, as a conglomerate of human beings and also as individuals, we are not taking advantage of one of the main attributes that distinguish us from animals, we are not planning, we are not preventing, we are not investing labor to build, to order, to build, to dominate nature and to benefit from its strength. What's going on? We let things happen.

As a conclusion

January 17, 2016

And then what, what's the point?

The point is that Labor is Capital.

In the productive process, the laborer does not contribute his labor force, they contributes their labor.

The wage that they receives must be an advance of the retribution obtained by their labor when it is realized as merchandise.

How does this become possible? Well, there is a lot of maths to be done, a new accounting is required.

Whoever has read this will realize that laying the foundations of a new economy, even modifying the conditions of production, is a task for interdisciplinary active groups.

*
* *

References

[1] Rick BILLSTEIN, Shlomo LIBESKIND, and Johnny LOTT. *A Problem Solving Approach to Mathematics for Elementary School Teachers*. 12th. Pearson, 2016. URL: http://bit.ly/2vGbgbg (visited on 05/05/2019).

[2] M. ILIN and E. SEGAL. *How Man Became a Giant*. English. Trans. Russian by Beatrice KINKEAD. 1945. URL: https://archive.org/details/howmanbecameagia035496mbp/page/n7 (visited on 05/05/2019).

[3] Karl MARX. *Das Kapital. Kritik der politischen Oekonomie*. English. Ed. and trans. German by Hans G. EHRBAR. Vol. I. Hamburg: Otto Meisner, 1867. URL: http://content.csbs.utah.edu/~ehrbar/cap1.pdf (visited on 05/05/2019).

[4] George PÓLYA. *How to Solve It*. Princeton, NJ: Princeton University Press, 1945. URL: http://press.princeton.edu/titles/669.html.

Index

A

around, 9

C

Cabos
  Los, 37
Cancun, 37
capital, 11, 24
Chimalapas, 1
chocolate
  Oaxaca and, 50
circle, 9
classists, 28
Coast, 1
compost, 47
computer
  technology, 18
concepts
  evolución of, 42
concession, 36
conclusion
  as a, 56
conjecture, 52
cosmopolitan, 28
counterexample, 52

D

deductive
  reasoning, 5
destiny
  Mexico's?, 28
development, 38
dictatorship, 34
Did The Future Reach Us?, 54

E

economy, 34
egalitarian, 28
employee
  and employer, 13
employer, 13
enjoying, 1
environment
  and us, 20
evolution
  of concepts, 42
exclusionary, 28
expropriate, 24

expropriation, 36

F
future
    did reach us?, 54

G
garbage
    waste and, 46

H
history, 1
horizontal
    and vertical, 44
Huatulco, 37
Huave, 1
humanist
    formation, 26

I
inductive reasoning, 52
Isthmus, 1

K
knowledge, 32

L
labor, 1, 3, 24
    and capital, 11
    and power, 9
    human, 7
    wage, 2

M
marginality, 38

MARX, KARL, 7
math teachers
    ed, 5, 15
    update, 29
mathematics, 5
    updating in, 6
merchandise, 34
Mixteca, 1
Moon
    water on the, 40
Moor, The, 7

N
1968, 22, 26

O
Oaxaca, 50, 54

P
plot
    against Mexico, 26
point, 9
preface, vii
proofreaders, 17

R
racists, 28
reasoning
    deductive, 5
    inductive, 52
royalties, 33, 34

S
Saturday, 5, 15, 29, 52
skills, 32

state, 24
straight, 9

T
tamales, 5
teachers, 6
30 years later, 22, 26
transformation, 9
typos, 17

U
uneducated, 28
update
    math teachers, 29

updating
    in mathematics, 6

V
vertical
    horizontal and, 44

W
waste
    and garbage, 46
water, 48
    on the Moon, 40
work
    community, 2

www.ingramcontent.com/pod-product-compliance
Lightning Source LLC
Chambersburg PA
CBHW030018190526
45157CB00016B/3110